Bubble Fusion

Danielle Wong

Bubble Fusion by Danielle Wong
© 2018 Danielle Wong

Publisher: Prairie Dragon Publishing
Editors: Melinda Cochrane and Danielle Wong
Cover Design: Ben Di Nunzio
ISBN: 978-0-9952863-1-3

Prairie Dragon Publishing

Legal Deposit-Bibliothèque et Archives nationales du Québec, 2018
Library and Archives of Canada, 2018

Acknowledgement

This book is possible because of a special group of people in my life. To my husband for his support while I was busy with this book. To my children for their inspiration and encouragement. To my sister for always being herself. To all my friends who have cheered me on over the years; I would not have been able to do this without your unconditional acceptance and encouragement. To Jodi Thiboutot for teaching my daughter the world of dance, bringing her out of her shell, and introducing me to Melinda Cochrane, a wonderful editor who knows how to get these poems out of me and into a book. Thanks for believing in me, Melinda. To Ben Di Nunzio for the wonderful artwork. To all the educators who worked with my daughter over the years, thank you.

Acknowledgements

Table of Contents

INSIDE AN UN-SUSPECTING BUBBLE.............. 47

Inside One Bubble

Babies are small when they are born. We expect them to grow at a certain rate. Sometimes a tiny baby does not follow that pace; the baby stays tiny not for several months, but for several years.

HELLO

Beautiful eyes sparkled bright,
giddy excitement bounced with a hurried
wake-up-wake-up-come-play-with-me
wrapped up and delivered with a smile,
never letting go,
present at every turn.

Day and Night

Sleepiness prevails.
Eating: effort is too great.
Soothed by rumble's song.

EVOLUTION

Tiny fingers
tiny hands
tiny body
strength un-bounding
strength un-foreseen
strength beyond years
age un-predictable
age un-calculable
age mysterious to outsiders
growth in time
growth when ready
growth external and internal
extension of us
extension of herself
extension of the world to come

BABY GYM UN-TOUCHED

Stare at the ceiling.
Deep in thought.
Jump at the doorbell.
Jump at a cough.
Hyperventilate.
One blink.
Relax.
Deep breath.
Stare at the ceiling.

SWIMMING POOLS

Voices echoed and bounced off walls;
a steady slapping of the water resounded,
miniature lightning.

Lights shone brightly;
whistles shrilled from time to time,
screeching through her body,
forcing her to bury herself in the arms
of her current protector.

Blood curdling screams escaped her
upon the sight
of the change we think slight
of dry to wet.

Soothed by voice,
terrified by sight;
confusion reigned.

FACES

Recognize faces,
must be exactly the same;
difference makes strangers.

FEEDING

Suckling difficult.
Bottles slightly easier.
Life-giving milk seemed to weaken.
Soy milk always welcomed strength.
Two at twelve, the greatest achievement.
Close eyes.
Sleep some more.

ACTIVITY CENTRE

She sat in her crib
and smiled while she watched her mom.
There was a new box.

A center of games:
overwhelming torture, grief,
brought blood-curdling cries

and paralysis
until all covered, but one;
happiness returned.

9

FIRST ART DAY

Brightly coloured paper,
tiny pieces, different shapes,
stayed on the table;
wanted to be picked up,
wanted to be glued down
in one pattern or another.

Brightly coloured paper,
tiny pieces, different shapes,
stayed on the table;
gathered dust, gathered time,
gathered despair, no understanding.
Un-expected sticky drop and spread.

Brightly coloured paper,
tiny pieces, different shapes,
tiny fisted blizzard
forcibly spread around,
flattened with steamroller strength
in a momentary furious frenzied focus.

STAIRWELL LULLABY

chopstick
stairwell
this step
that step
chop chopstick
stairwell
this step
that step
chop chopstick
stairwell
this this step
that step
chop chopstick
chop chopstick
chop chop
chop chop
chop chopstick
chop

MEALTIME

Arms out   spin
Arms in   spin
Arms out   spin
Arms in   spin
So many smells outside, inside food cooking
Arms out   spin   and twirl
Arms in   spin   and twirl
Arms out   spin   and twirl
Arms in   spin   and twirl
Table fills up with glasses, forks, knives, spoons, napkins,
plates, bowls, food.
So much to look at.
So many smells.
Jump off the chair.
Escape to the next room.
Spin   twirl   spin   spin
Spin   twirl   spin   spin
Spin   twirl   spin   spin
Spin   twirl   spin   spin
The dull glitter of the spoon with food is the north pole that
she must repel by her very nature.
Spin   twirl   spin   spin
Spin   twirl   spin   spin
Mouth clenched shut.

Spin	twirl	spin	spin
Spin	twirl	spin	spin
Spin	twirl	spin	spin

Catch her from behind and tickle her jaw open with the tip of one finger and the baby bird's mouth opens just enough to drop in food with the other fingers.

Spin	twirl	spin	spin
Spin	twirl	spin	spin
Spin	twirl	spin	spin
Spin	twirl		
Spin	twirl		
Spin	twirl		
Spin			

Lego Music

Red,
blue, yellow,
white, black, tan,
single ones, single twos, single threes,
foursies, sixsies, eights, long by twos, green bases, red
bases, doors, windows, wheels, hundreds more, hundreds
more clink, clang, clatter, jangle, smack, slap
onto the floor.

Smile.
Joy absorbed from ears to toes.
Hands swim through to create a
clinking, clangour, jangle, clatter of hundreds of dollars
worth of coins in a plastic bag shaken and shaken and
shaken.
The floor has disappeared.

It lies hidden under
wheels, windows, doors, red bases, green bases, long by
twos, eights, sixsies, foursies,
single threes, single twos, single ones,
tan, black, white,
yellow, blue,
red.
She walks away.

COMFORTS

blankets:
great to suck on.
TV tables, foot of beds:
great to chew on.
toys, ballpoint pens, erasers:
what all meals should be made of.

OPENING PORTS

No
word answers:
smile
ignore.
One
word answers:
yes
no.
Tan and white:
puppy
puppet
invades
her space.
"Talk to me! Or I'll talk to you!"
Slowly,
sunrise by sunrise,
moon rise by moon rise,
puppy puppet confidant,
sentry of secrets,
becomes the portal
between two universes.

BIRD LEARNING TO FLY

They stood at the top.
One by one
to the bottom they slid.
Impatient,
or overwhelmed by the crowd,
she flew
over the edge and down.
Graceful flight.
She dusted off the sand.
No tears.
She pondered what to do,
then climbed
back
up to the top.

CUTLERY

Father	mother
Brother	sister
Boy	girl
Big fork	little fork
Big spoon	little spoon

little fork
She eats only with a little fork,
little spoon.
The masculine obstructs nourishment.

SIRENS

Sirens call,
begging attention.
Drop toys.
Walk away.
Get to the window.
Crouch.
Eyes above sill.
Eyes grow wide,
excited.
Red firetruck.
Yellow ambulance.
White police car.
Red firetruck.
All zoom by
together,
alone.
Slink
      to
         the
            floor.
            Close eyes.
            Crawl
                away.

GARBAGE TRUCKS

Dinosaur garbage trucks
roar many blocks away.
Run to the window,
wait for them to show their
hulking bodies and their
beady eyes, mouths in back.
Dreaded excitement
knowing they keep coming.
Share leftover food;
keeps them from eating us.
They roll into full view.
Hide below windowsill.
Safety in mom's bedroom.
Roar past all the houses.
Slink to the floor.
Will they come the other way?
Or leave until another day?

PRESENT

Choice: Christmas present
one red, two-wheeled bicycle;
her only desire.

COUNTING SOUNDS

Sirens
loud and clear
a distant storm
only she can say
how many are police cars
how many are speeding firetrucks
how many are blocked ambulances
giving updates by the minute
tension growing as they near
storm is raging through her
hide under blankets
storm passes by
hush, my dear,
breathe.

CROSSING ROOMS

There's comfort
in staying where you are.
There's desire
in being over there.
Close eyes;
imagine you are there.
Stand up;
walk over to that place.
Other people:
manoeuver around them.
Open eyes;
you made it safe and sound.

Telepathy Should Be the Norm

Ask a simple question.
Lock eyes.
Silence fills the room.
She gets up.
No answer ever uttered.
Carry on.
The answer floats in her bubble.
Realize.
We should read each other.
Maintain.
Great peace and tranquility.

RIDES

Learn in the basement
doing tiny, circus circles;
the start of riding.

Go for a bike ride.
Sights and sounds pounce and torment.
Stop. Throw bike in road.

Tired from the school day;
escape it all; bike away.
Down hill is best.

Too hot. Too tired now.
Can never go fast enough.
Take the car; drive far away.

Circle Time

Do not push.
Do not rush.
Do not ask.
I'm not on your timetable.

I am sweet.
I am kind.
I am fast.
I will speak when I'm ready.

I am wrath.
I am fury.
Tornado.
Remove everyone.
Remove everything.
Remove frustrations
that lie upon my skin.

Calm. Corner.
Soothed by books:
size and texture, smell and taste;
meaning is overlooked.

30-SECOND LESSONS

Sit

in a chair
and listen is too hard to stop moving toes, feet, legs,
fingers, hands, arms. Sit

in a chair
and listen to a voice that is too near when the drill three
blocks away grinds away at the wood while someone farther
away hammers and a police car drives by

Slide
  under
   the
    table
     and
       finally

hear the person beside you tell you something seemingly
important but within 30 seconds the words start to melt
one into the other and it all turns into the same background
noise that was there when first told to sit

in a chair.

END OF SCHOOL DAY

Spent the day at school.
Too many people. That noise!
Throw shoes. Scream. Mom's fault.

Airplanes

round and blue
bounce and roll
lie down
face down
legs straight out
finally fun
throw socks of rolled-up socks
through hula-hoop holes
one and one more and more
giggle and laugh
too tired to do more
roll off
lie down
universe
finally
calm

MOUSE CLICKS

Where to click?
Where to click?
Click here
and click there.
Nothing's happening!
Click here.
Click there. Click here and here and here.
Network freeze.

Un-freeze.
Where to click?
Did she say click here? Did she say click there?

Click here
and here and here and here here here here.
Breathing short.

She took my mouse!
I kicked.
She took my hands
behind my back,
wrapped a hair elastic over my wrists.

Compressed.
Feels good.
Deep breaths

finally!

Un-tied.
No mouse yet.
Her finger is on the screen.
One
click
left.
Aim
for
that
finger.
Click.
Done.
Screen changes.
Tired now.

1 + 1 = 17

Sumerians handed down a gift.
Babylonians attempted to do the same.
The base of circles, their music, and time
seemed to them a simple game.

Binary, ternary, quaternary
cannot fully explain the circle of the sun
or how seconds, minutes, hours, and months
can build on each other and make time run.

Sumerians handed down this gift.
A few are born with an innate sexagesimal thought
making one plus one seventeen correct,
but, in a decimal world, the answer not sought.

SAME VS DIFFERENT

Two circles
side by side.
One black.
One white.
They're different.

Two circles
side by side.
One has a box.
One has a line.
They're different.

Two circles
side by side.
One is red.
One is red.
They're different.

Same?
No.
Different.
One is here.
One is there.
That makes them
as different
as day is
to night.

READING, NOT READING

Words
on a page
are magical.
They bounce
here   and   there.
They play
hide and seek
when you get close.
They flip
                                         back to front,
front to back,
                        top
                                to
                                        bottom,
                                                bottom
                        to
                top.
Catch one
if you can;
it will tell you
a secret.
Catch them all;
words are collectibles.
Catch them all;
you're a trainer,
eventually gym leader.

But that drains
your energy,
your pokedex battery,
your pokeball.
Best
to set them
all free
and enjoy
the clatter they make
on the turn
of every
page.

CROSSING OUTDOORS

Focus: destination.
Aware: noisy.
monstrous
beasts
everywhere.
Refocus: destination.
Stand up.
Open eyes.
Shut down sight.
Hit by monstrosity.
Brush it off.
Annoyed.
Destination: arrived.

CROSSING THE STREET

Cross the street.
Simple enough
when nothing is out there.
Roaring truck's down the street,
six or seven blocks away
at the top of that mountainous hill.
Cannot escape that feeling,
cannot escape the urge:
drop down to the ground,
round like a ball.
Go away.

NEW MEANS NOT ALL

New rules
New place
New smiles
New faces
No choice
No relief
No hiding
No belief
All changes
All equal
All faces
All spaces

STUDENT STRIKE

They are everywhere
with their diaphragm
laughter, cat calls, anger
demanding to be heard,
wishing take notice.
Their eyes take hold
and slide down my arm,
back, front, face, and legs.
They shoot out their arms
forcing their paper.
I need to escape
to my yellow world.
Panic trips me up.
The start of the end
begins with my blood
and changing my face.
I hold in the tears.
No one notices
my mind and bag
crushed.

TRAVELLING NEAR AND FAR

How many places
are un-familiar;
each time we insist
they are familiar.
Odors are un-known,
as are all the sights;
over simplify,
smells and sights are known.
This is not my bed
nor is it your own.
Tonight, it is my bed
and you have your own.
Cupboard's bowls and cups:
beautiful rainbow.
Waterfall swing set.
Thunder strikes. Run. Hide.
Inside hood. Can't eat.
All that's familiar
is un-known to me.

TRYING TO FIT IN

Awkward confusion shared
among an entire class
a few classes a day;
perhaps now there's friendship.
Arguments start to flow.
My interests are not theirs.
The one I need to guide me
hides her secrets from me.
I drown while manoeuvering
my old dreams, these people.
They say it's important.
This is completely wrong.
This world is not my world.
This world has no freedom.
Heart and soul should fly free.
Stop all this awkward confusion.

CHANGE PROGRAMS

Open blossom. Bloom.
Another element here.
Stomped on by their words.

How Can Communication Be Possible?

Words are confusing
with their height, width, and depth.
Interchange syllables
and the meaning is left
incomprehensibly
comprehensible
to a large group adept
in the art of growing words
from that blasted alphabet.

ROLLERCOASTER

                    Storms rage,
un-controlled,
                                        un-controllable.
                    Need to shout,
find hurtful words;
                                        use these swords
on everyone nearby.
                    Thunder claps.
Fear fills up.
Sun shines all around.

                                        Momentarily.

Clouds build up.
                    Storms rage.

RETREAT TO THE BUBBLE

Jump and twirl, and go, go, go
changed, transformed, to slow, slow, slow.
Much too tired to move about;
the couch a favourite lookout.
Retreat inside the bubble;
video screens less trouble
than dealing with all of them;
that's where all the problems stem.
Retreat inside this bubble.
Stop waterfall's rumble.
Replace attempts to try, try, try
with a silent bye, bye, bye.

Inside an Un-suspecting Bubble

Every person is different. Every person sees things in a unique light.
Every person experiences life in a way no one else can. In spite of
all our differences, a sense of familiarity exists among us all.

RIVER WITHIN

Waves crashed,
trying to free the silt
from its invisible world,
succeeding to spray
a few drops on my surface;
communicating
reality, a failure.
Frustrated fury
coursed underneath my skin
clutching at my heart,
relentlessly keeping hold,
squeezing from my lungs
a maintained desire for laughter.
All good intentions,
alien to this universe,
wanting to be heard
cannot breach the gap where
waves crashed.

CONTINUAL TRAIN OF THOUGHT

Familiar   sensed un-familiar
Confusion   sought clarity
Requested   explanation
Informed   it will all be fine
Confusion   something is different
Silence   brought about worry
Requested   information
My un-known   their first suspicion

DAY 280

Come fast
Come quick
Speed is of the essence
My breath
Your breath
Withheld by un-seen forces
Bruised blue
Breath blue
I cannot hold you
I slip
You fade
Struggle after struggle
I cry
You cry
Two snow globes side by side

DON'T SAY A WORD

Blank stares
Silent coos
> Where are you?

Soft skin
Dark eyes
> Who's in there?

Call me
> with pounding feet
Raging growl
> weaker than sleep

Dark eyes
Soft skin
Silent coos
Blank stares
> I love you.

KANGAROOS

Baby kangaroo
wants sun instead of shade
wants shade instead of sun
wants to stay near the pouch
wants to stay in the pouch
Mama kangaroo
accommodates

GROWTH

Textbooks can drown
or trickle like a dry stream.
Textbooks can dampen
all sense of ability.
Textbooks can inhabit
the stagnation of mind and body.
Textbooks are responsible
for nothing in how we grow.

EATING TABLES

Beautiful smile
throbbing pain behind eyes
up on lap
cradle in my arms
feet to the sky
mouth wide open
push down grief
gently pull splinter
rub gum gently
set free.
What did I do wrong?

DISCONNECTING

full term   preemie
6 months   newborn
1 year   puppet, doll
                    words lose meaning
                        minds made up
                    losing battles
                        already judged
                    losing connections
            self-righteous, omniscient

                    nowhere to turn

FORMS

Ask me about my child.
Observations and quirks
I list on the paper.
They read it over,
laugh out loud to my face.
All exaggeration;
they claim it can't be true.
Overprotective mom.
Each word I said was true.
I tried to re-explain.
Their look of disbelief
said they'd never believe
no matter how I told
our reality, our truth.
Why am I giving them
my child while I work all day?
Trigger childhood pain:
adults eradicating
all my words and thoughts
that spoke my reality.

BUILDING EXHAUSTION

Tears of laughter
hide exhaustion
from rule after rule
rectified and reconciled
with those of the tiny world
that collided with this universe.
Rules of twirls,
rules of spins,
caught and restarted,
refueled the rocket.
Rules of only red cups,
rules of girl spoons,
rules of girl forks
supplied with a smile
circumvented screams
and tight-mouthed refusal
to let anything pass
through the gateway
without uttering magic words,
without providing a magic twinkle behind your eyes,
without waving the magic signal that is your smile.

HOW WAS THIS ASSISTANCE?

Pulled aside,
hushed tones,
dirty secrets
already known:
food intake
near non-existent.
Specialist can help
with their white coats.
Time of day is poorly chosen,
chosen without my say.
She finally starts,
forced to stop.
Meal taken away.
Cookies provided.
Confusion on the tiny face.
She halts.
Perplexed.
Exasperated.
Trapped.
Windowed room.
Child being watched,
un-nerving and un-doing
all motherly instincts;
every move made
too fast, too slow, insufficient, too much.
Screams from the back seat
un-bearable

at the passing of giant buildings -
all look suspicious -
at basic paint smocks -
worn by every art teacher.
Damage done.
Damage permanent.
Child,
mother
broken.

MULTI VS MONO

Try to teach children
in a must buy society
material goods

not really required;
hold human interaction
higher and above.

Criticized for this,
harsh words and impatience reigned.
Christmas wish too small:

one red bicycle;
her heart desired this one thing,
wondered how to ride.

Message: not enough.
Close-minded mono-cultural
was all I could see.

Clashing of values,
my shield came up to protect
more harm on its way.

She finally could eat;
who cares about the spin, spin, twirl?
We're not all the same.

Daggers thrown at me
grazed my skin, cut the upper left
corner of my heart.

My life was changing:
mistrust of all strangers grew.
I know my daughter

past, present family:
secrets and keys are in there.
We just need to breathe.

PRIME COLOURS

Words of abstraction
        are hard to describe
        are hard to pinpoint
        are hard to explain
Look through my cupboard
        what do I have there
        what can be useful
        what will be helpful
Four prime-coloured cups
        water in red
        water in blue
        water in yellow
Hours spent at the sink
        pour into green
        pour into yellow
        pour into red
Slow and then faster
        red into blue
        blue into red
        red into green
Feet ache, heart aches
        green back to red
        red goes into blue
        blue back to red

Every single day
        red goes to yellow
        yellow back to red
        empty all the cups
Several times a day
        water in the blue
        blue goes to yellow
        yellow goes to green
Laughing, getting wet
        green pours to red
        yellow pours to red
        blue pours to red

SENSING INEVITABLE PHONE CALLS

Focus.
Try to focus.
Try to get some work done.
Did they believe a word I said?
Did they heed my warning labels and caution signs?

Recess.
Pins and needles
I sit and hesitate;
skip the coffee break down the hall.
The phone call lassoes my ankles, throws me down hard.

A calf
now lies helpless.
My mawing is finally heard,
her mawing has shattered one young heart,
a shower of intervention pours down from the sky.

Switch rooms.
Grandma has the strength
to laugh and find the switch
or enter momentarily,
connect to her world if only for a moment.

Reason:
great messenger
between two different worlds
though neither one can understand
what the other is trying to get across, lost in space's void.

SPEAK TO ME

Love that turn of her head
mischievous smile
her favourite word
monosyllabic no

Love that puppy puppet
found at the store
cuddle each night
follows her everywhere

Puppet's annoying voice
entry point
to her bubble
learn how she is thinking

Night after night bedtime
secrets told
about her world
vocabulary grows

Puppet's conversation
excited
I am not there
puppet's identity

Fractioning: in pieces
she's speaking
we're all learning
I'm becoming someone else

(Dis)agree

first time	not so.
around kids.	four years.
won't play	she plays
with them.	with siblings.
can't be.	it's true
no sign.	quirky,
certain	sideway looks
different	block all
reactions.	chances.
make her	make them

change

JUDGEMENTS

I gave birth to an anorexic thing, not a baby
> silent, tiny, weary child lies in my arms most of the day

I'm overfeeding junk food to the oldest
> bites into onions and lemons like apples, cheese a daily joy

I'm mysteriously stunting height of the second
> ancestry is tall and short, growth spurts often quite late

I'm obviously ignoring and neglecting the third
> sleepless nights and days, waking, coaxing to eat, protecting,
> playing

I never sent my child to daycare before school
> husband took them every day, I picked them up after
> spending my day at work

I must have raised my child to be like this
> confusion reigns why there are few responses,
> sadness at outbursts

I have no right to ask anyone for help
> exhausted broken heart retreat silently to my bubble, please
> leave me alone

FIRST DAY

Fear fills me
when I see
children run,
climb on toys,
teachers stand,
adults smile.
My fear,
her fear,
intertwined,
she hangs on,
clutching me
gorilla
style, and I
force myself
request help:
separate us.
Regret eats
my tired brain.
Hold back tears.
Hold back run
back to her.
Tell me lies.
She'll be fine.
This is good:
yes and no.
Doubt fills me.

Why do I
dare do this
to someone
like her?

WAITING OUT

Rifles
and machine guns shot
a barrage of words
that I dodged as long as I could.

Shrapnel
dug its way under
my skin. Deep breaths
and obedience led me to

ridicule
even when I
managed to head down
two paths at once.

Twelve months of flower-ripping
and lumberjacking my home.
Definition gave
more questions
than answers.

BURY EMOTIONS

Never get angry
Stay calm at all times
Wise words of advice
Told repeatedly
Bury emotions
Explain and explain
Explain and explain
Explain and explain
No one understands
Lock myself up
Scream and cry, repeat
Head throbs from head butts
One more time concussed
Never examined
Frustration rises
Lock myself up
Scream and cry, repeat
Energy drains
Keep up the charade
In front of children
In front of adults
Stay calm at all times
Never get angry

Hindrance: Information

Book upon book,
print out upon print out,
pour on top of me.

Pages cut me.
Absorb word after word,
dictionary

my best friend
for supposedly simply
written prose.

Doubt creeps in,
beats me with each passing word.
Misunderstood?

Do words mislead?
Their meaning everywhere.
Splitting apart,

I look left,
I look right.
Same straight sight.

No sense,
no logic
can compute,
can rectify
my universe
with the world of these words.

WORK BLENDS WITH HOME

Focus:
>either too strong or not there

Muscles:
>twitch with spiders trapped under skin

Jump:
>every telephone ring and touch on shoulder

Tachycardia:
>balance worries and changed expectations

Paranoia:
>eyes watch you, disapprove choices

Employment:
>permanently temporary, demand more than can
>>give

Instability:
>from work leads to home

Failure:
>both professionally and in birth

NEWS

Grim Reaper came and sat down beside me
the day they said she'd never really read.
He put his frigid hand on my shoulder.
I tried un-clutching his tightening grip.
Satanic laughter roared from his belly.
His eyes attempted to suck her knowledge.
He breathed heavy icicles in my ear.
He planted seeds of doubt and un-certainty.
I pushed him down to avert his stare.
He stood up, rapier in hand, and flew off,
part of me with him in the otherworld.

MASSAGES

Push down anxiety
brush too hard
brush too light
absorb her wrath
towards me

Push down all my fear
compress her
decompress
head butt, knee in face
hug near

Painful waves rush through me
she hugs me
I hug her
we kiss, cuddle
and laugh

Alterations

Metal from cars melt
invisibly
the simplest touch
sneaks in the bloodstream
eats your existence
the robot takes over
smile when expected
give all the correct answers
cold metal touches the heart
a battle ensues
will true emotions live or die?

AFTER SCHOOL DRIVE HOME

Prophecy fulfilled
She throws her shoe at my head.
Am I that bad a mom?

MONDAY TO FRIDAY

Homework times two
intersperse
with obstacle courses
yoga ball airplanes
make dinner in between
nothing gets done
nothing is ready
un-able to think straight
un-able to hold back tears at work
I'm failing at everything.

BOOKS

Scientist
Mom
Sit back
Observe
Want to pull her from her bubble
Book size matters
She does love her books
Books for the floor
Books for the hand
Please don't take a nibble
Favourite books devoured
That was a first edition, 1951
Interesting
I'm losing my precious gems

LOOKING FOR REASON

Sleepless night
Sleepless day
Rethink birth
Cord collapsed
I failed her
Cord wrapped round
It strangled her
Silent
Blue
Burning seared me
How did I cause this?

SUMMER STORMS

Sky lights up; musical drum rolls bang
Happy memories of candlelit card games
Calming effect on mind, body, and soul
One step toward the window, I get pulled back
Screams of fear fill the house, shirt pulled on, hard
Hands and legs climb me; mama gorilla
Walk away; hid under sweaters, blankets
Hear in the distance family oo's and ah's
Every single summer storm spent like this
Each time losing one more piece of memories
Resentment settles in, segregated
Forsaken, cast away, make life elsewhere
Content self with hiding at the first sight
Joyless resignation, exhale all dreams
Entry point, portal, start to close off
Move into her bubble thoroughly
Two snow globes into a single one
Forget what was once there in present, past
Dread the oncoming music and light show
Candlelit card games blown out, goodbye mom
Relinquish music, don't look to the sky

SCHOOL MEETINGS

Round table
Oval table
Square table
Rec-table
Smiles all around
agendas
hidden among lines
on paper
hidden among lines
on faces
hidden among words
that fall out
They know best
one person
among hundreds
I don't
one person
among finger count
Eyes smile
Eyes bore
Eyes avert
Eyes speak
contradict
sounds made
all voices
same time
one after

another
confuse
my ears
confuse
my eyes
confuse
I can't tell
Each year
the same
gets worse
spoken words
lose all meaning
computation
all wrong
all years
escape
through salted
storms
They stare
I'm nuts
no good
to be blamed
for this whole life
Solution
they know
Solution
I don't

Solution
each day
I know less

VISITING THE ZOO

Picnic basket
Kids in the car
Excitement bubbles up

Exotic sights
Exotic smells
A day of casual walk

Giraffes stand tall
Long legs stretch out
Eat leaves from the tree top

Drop to the ground
Run down the path
There's no stopping to look

Find a playground
Swing on the swings
The others explore the zoo

Run down the paths
Do not lose sight
Misplaced child my nightmare

Find a wood bench
Sit in the shade
Exotic sound un-nerve

Vague memories
Un-funded zoo
Have to hang on to those

Exotic sights
Exotic smells
Not mine to discover

Heavy eyes close
Breathe in deeply
I've been spilt on the bench

Hold back thoughts
Say nothing
They complain how I look

Wish I could see
All that they saw
Maybe next year; probably not

THE CRACK

Two fused snow globes crack.
Hail attacks and breaks the glass.
I feel out of reach.

PERHAPS

Perhaps if I were better
as a worker, mom, adult
whatever's been thrown at me
would bounce and slip to the floor.

Perhaps if I were better
as a student, teenager, child
their eyes and words would not cut
my soul, her soul; sour this life.

Perhaps if I were better
I'd find a better way out;
no bubbles, no pain, no hurt
for her, for me, everyone.

Perhaps if I were better
I'd have the strength I need;
from this book erase us both:
that strength is not found in me.

PENDULUM

Pendulum swings
     side to side
          its path between
               un-seen.

                    Avoid the swings
               cringe and brace
        the up, the down
     don't drown

Ignore the swings
     smile and hug
          yet cry inside
               please hide

                    Pendulum swings
               black to white
        Pendulum swings
     white to black

Pendulum swings

                    Pendulum swings

Pendulum swings

          good night

TRYING TO ESCAPE

Flip through emails
don't read
Flip through posts
don't read
Flip through news
don't read
Floor plans
one bedroom
Floor plans
one kitchen
Floor plans
one debt
Flip through emails
Flip through posts
Flip through news
Floor plans
Floor plans
Floor plans
Reality check
Two bedrooms
Three bedrooms
Four

CHIT CHAT

Did you see that show last night?
Did you watch that movie?
Head shake and silence.
Listen to them all agree
on this part and that part.
Sit and listen and
retreat to my bubble.
Segregate myself.
Return and pay attention
stand back and observe.
I'm a left open-toed shoe
among pairs and pairs of sneakers.

TILTED BALANCE

Work is a noose around my neck.
Load is the guillotine.
Kids are the chains that keep me here,
tethering me to this world.

WHEN THE DAM BREAKS

Hold it back.
Hold it in.
Wear the mask
tight.
Bit by bit
swelling starts.
Mask cracks.
Can't hold it back.
Can't hold it in.
Don't understand peers.
Don't understand other kids.
Dam doesn't patch.
Dam lets water loose.
Let them stare.
Let them whisper.
I don't care anymore.
I can't care anymore.
Segregated.
Separated.
I left their world.
They won't let me back in.
Too hard
in theirs
in hers
in mine.
Start over.

If only I could
run from them,
run from me.
It would be a run
for eternity.

HALF WAITING

Head out in the morning
Sit down at my desk
Half wait for the phone call
That makes me drop and go

Give her a mid-day hug
Tip upside-down, recenter
Head back to the office
Sit down at my desk

Half wait for the phone call
That makes me drop and go
Find out what just happened
Make appointments, make repairs

Head back to our home
Half wait for a fall out
Cuddle on the couch
Learn about triggers

Get them off to bed
Stories, laughter resound
Head to my own room
Half wait for alarm clock

Middle of the night
Wake up, make up hours
Sit down at my desk
Half wait for the voice call

That makes me drop and go
Hug, lie down beside bed
Reassure all is fine
Head back down the stairs

Sit down at my desk
Half wait for the alarm clock
That makes me drop and go
Get family going

Head out now it's morning
Sit down at my desk
Half wait for the phone call
That makes me drop and go

DAILY RIVER

Socialize
with peers over lunch
increasingly
quite illogical
different worlds
that don't understand
best to run
down to the river
slip my feet
into the cold water
watch the sky
seagulls, ducks fly by
breathe in waves
let go of the job
breathe in waves
let go of the house
listen well
my heart speaks to me
survive
job all wrong for me
capable
can't think fast enough
want to quit
must support family
go walk back
don't see car coming
someone's hand

holds me back and looks
I am numb
accept but I don't
his kind act
I'm muddled inside

CLOUDS ABOVE MY HEAD

Thunderclouds followed me
right above my head.
Their weight, incredible,
I could not ignore.

Scream them all away.
They'd return time again.
Machete through the fog.
Black hole is all I found.

Time Ticks Inside Bubbles

Life always throws dark shadows over time. The trick is to throw them off and see what is really underneath.

Pick Up, Please

Places: bus, train, stop
Shoes come off,
stay on the floor
Love her company

SMALL BREAKS

Cry from exhaustion
soot on the family room floor
clouded by it all

Chickpeas, rice, lentils
scattered on the kitchen floor
sounds filling her needs

He sees the flood
gives me oars for the next week
it's all he can do

I paddle away
foreign sounds wash over me
land on an island

Segregated, alone
isolation in the crowd
two hours, recenter

ORAL TRADITIONS

bedtime
storytime
lights go out
restless souls
wound up from

bedtime
storytime
tell some more
random thoughts
strung together

bedtime
storytime
giggles and laughs
wants to re-hear
a calming voice

bedtime
storytime
the voice drifts off
rhythmic breathing and snores
shower the room with stardust.

THE PLAY

She clings to the shadows:
hides from the eyes.

She wears an evening dress:
confidence on stage.

She hunts for security:
mom, dad, puppy puppet.

She plays the part of mom:
eyesight failing.

She bows, jumps off stage:
perfect performance.

SHOE LACES

Left lace over right lace.
Right lace over left.
Try again when older.

Left lace over right lace.
Right lace over left.
Try again when older.

Left lace over right lace.
Knot made.
What's next?

Left rabbit ear.
Right rabbit ear.
You're kidding!

One rabbit ear.
Lace circles around.
No way!

Left lace over right.
Right lace over left.
Giggle. Don't look.

Floppy bow.
Only one shoe.
Foot falls out.

Left lace over right.
Right lace over left.
Rabbit ears.

Left rabbit ear.
One lace runs around.
Sneak into the rabbit hole.

Left foot.
Right foot.
Volunteer to fix all laces.

TELEPHONE

Tuesday night, telephone call:
slide to the floor, eyes closed,
hands fused to the chest,
mouth sealed lip to lip.

Tuesday night, telephone call:
slide to the floor, eyes closed,
hand holds receiver to ear,
mouth sealed lip to lip.

Tuesday night, telephone call:
slide to the floor, eyes closed,
hand holds receiver to ear,
mouth sealed, head nods yes, no.

Tuesday night, telephone call:
slide to the floor, eyes closed,
hand holds receiver to ear,
mouth opens, answer yes, no.

Tuesday night, telephone call:
stand by the phone, eyes closed,
hand holds receiver to ear,
mouth opens, answer yes, no.

Tuesday night, telephone call:
stand by the phone, eyes open,
hand holds receiver to ear,
words spill out fast, excited.

Tuesday night, telephone call:
stand by the phone, eyes closed,
rush to dial the number first,
words spill out fast, excited.

Tuesday night, telephone, cell:
sit on the couch, text friends,
thumbs dance across the letters,
laughter bounces off the walls.

DISTRACTIONS

I'm trapped in a chair
monotone noise surrounds me
escape and retreat

imagine bubbles
float above everyone's head
self-entertainment

pseudo dictation
keep track of important points
must pay attention

colliding bubbles
crash above everyone's head
dance of distractions

notes gain a new form
disconnected words
lines down, lines across

draw on paper bubbles
thoughts rising from the water
new relaxation

FROM WATER IN CUPS

Prime coloured cups
lead to
prime coloured crayons
mixed with
prime coloured paint:
gouache, acrylic.
Prime coloured ideas
filled up
prime coloured paper
became
prime coloured canvases
that came
to live in the house
turned gallery

WASTING TIME

Confined to a metal box
heat bearing down
cold seeping in
time ticking away
reminding me of the schedule
wait at this bus stop
wait at that train station
wait in silence's
scream of un-intelligible ideas
soothing once un-leashed
birthed from breath
in scribblings in an old notebook

PASSING TOY BOATS

Shy waves caress my feet,
whisper distant stories,
remind me of past passions
pulling pen to paper
on short summer lunch hours;
true stories hidden in myths,
carried in and out by barges
floating alongside the shore,
penetrate every gray crevice,
ask politely every day, repeatedly,
to be given life, given breath,
in etchings along blue lines,
roads to ideas and mysterious paths.

MINISCULE MOMENT OF A MINISCULE MELODY

Melody with multiple words
sung every day,
sung every night.
Fingers of right hand learn.
Fingers of left hand learn.
Play from beginning to end
a miniscule piece
in a miniscule room
one time only
never again.
Warmed by the memory
played once, at least,
this melody of multiple words.

HANGING ON

Watch each word spoken
Avoid disapproving eyes
Create hidden universes
No one can see
Create life from bubble thoughts
Introduce one to the other
Whisper only to closest friends
Release the blackness growing
From outside

DOUBLE HAPPINESS

Bird songs fill the room
Can't help but smile at the sound
Her voice calms me down

SERIOUS PHOTOSHOOTS

Photoshoot
Favourite alternate voice
Multiple shots
Tan and white
Puppy puppet
A full album

CULMINATION OF YEARS

Pent up nervousness:
what will they say?
what will they do?
She can't cross a stage.
She can't read like them.
She can't count like them.
They can't think like her.
Every ounce of energy
used in counting,
used in reading,
used in standing up,
crossing the stage
Practice and rehearse.
Practice and rehearse.
Practice.
Rehearse.
On the final day
she walks across,
remembers hand shake,
runs to the stairs on the side,
proclaims with a wide smile,
"I did it!"

DANCING

Tiny teenager
in a tiny room
magical movement
in a music room
intricate ideas
in an idyllic room
that grew and changed
sudden and soon

Clutch and cling
quickly changed into
dance and spin
with friends all new
smile big grins
remembered each movement
confidence soars
over the moon

DINNER TIME

Look up from the food
laid on the table
sitting and pouting
sitting and smiling
sitting and talking
sitting across from me
sitting and eating
the whole meal

STOPWATCH

Crowded race
Not much time allowed
Lots to say

STORMS BRING SUNSHINE

Tornado wind brings
torrential rain.
Softly blown kiss brings
blue skies and sun.
Mention of friends brings
lemonade and lawn chairs.
Confidence blossoms:
bud opens slow, lasts long.

COLLECTIBLES

Line them up
side by side
from the table to the couch
from the couch to the piano
from the piano to the wall.

Row after row
of every colour
of every shade
some with glitter
some transparent.

No place left to walk
not much place to stand back
gawk in amusement
take photos from above
panoramic view insufficient.

Flop on the floor
for colourful close-ups
hundreds of shots
a quarter of these subjects
living in our home.

CARD GAMES

Coloured cards
Directions
Change directions
Confusion
Skip a turn
Sadness to overcome

Coloured cards
Directions
Change directions
Crazy times
Skip a turn
Scream with laughter

Coloured cards
Directions
Change directions
Can follow
Skip a turn
Silliness seen

First to lose cards
First to keep cards
Fun in all that comes first

Speaking Out Loud

They watched one movie,
read an article or two,
honestly believed in cookie cutters.
I told them the truth:
Range from one end to the other,
top to bottom.
We aren't that different.
We just think we are.
It's this I repeat and repeat.
Most walk away,
ears covered;
knowledge too much to bear.
Some dare to come close,
feel what it's like hour after hour,
learn how hard it is:
joy packed in minuscule boxes,
one step forward, five steps back, one forward.
Sensitized adults:
Dangerous sword once hurled
now dulled,
destroyed,
un-recognizable in the dump.
Invisible waves wash over me
as a throng of similar people
require more and more
to be understood
and heard.

Are You Okay?

Long day at work.
Deadlines shorten.
Workload increases.
Quietly hold it all in.
I feel empty,
nothing left to give.
She comes up to me.
A hand on my hand.
Outstretched arms ready to hug.
Her head on my shoulder.
Are you okay?
We breathe deeply

together.

SHOW THE SCRIBBLINGS OF THE HIDDEN REPLAY

Replay the looks
Replay the words
Replay what happened
Heart breaks

Hide in a room
Hide in a corner
Hide in a dark space
Heart leaks

Scribble in mind
Scribble on paper
Scribble in books
Heart heals

Show one more replay
Show what was hid
Show some scribblings
Heart set free

BLUEBIRD

Bluebird
Sing a song
Predators took your nest

Bluebird
Sing a song
Now you have nothing left

Bluebird
Flap your wings
Grab a breath and rest

Bluebird
Sing a song
Your flight is picturesque

NATURE

Lightning strikes
missing its target.
No flames burn.
Rumblings grow distant:
thunder,
buses
trains
further, further away.
Clouds thin.
Blue skies and sun
shine from her smile.
Newly found freedom.
Sprout has a growth spurt.
Reach the sky.
Grow permanent leaves.
Trunk straight,
strong.

POOLS

Week after week
Try and try again
Splish and splash
Walk with arms
Copy instructions
Enjoy the swim
Keep getting wet
Fear letting go
One day forget
Deep end
Do laps

Awareness Rising

She hands out harsh words.
Her hugs wash away the pain.
Now, she understands.

SHELTERS

Take shelter
Under tables
Strangers asking questions

Take shelter
Under bus seats
Strangers in cars cannot see

Take shelter
On bus seats
Make friends with bus drivers

Take shelter
At the stops
City bus, city train

Take shelter
In my arms
Hug at night, morning, too

Take shelter
In knowing
She gets herself places.

STORYTIME

Called to the bedroom
Bedtime routine
Big book on the bed
This time she reads
Pages filled with words
Children's books we love
Better than they said
And, yes, it was tough

PSEUDO-CRUSH

Night time
TV time
Always the same show
He's there
Talking
Misunderstanding friends
She smiles
She laughs
Her mind is made up
If must
Marry
He'd be her only one

QUIET HELP

Laundry basket on the table:
without a word she stands,
folds
shirts,
shorts,
skirts,
socks,
underwear
before vanishing to the couch.

DECIDE TO TRY

Hot summer day
Out of ice cream
She gathers coins from her wallet

She sits on the stairs
Texts for permission
To go outside for a short walk

She locks up the house
Walks to the small shop
Beside the bus stop she knows

She's faced with a choice
Ice cream, Mr.Freeze
She puts one on the countertop

Eyes everywhere else
She gives one coin
Just enough to pay for her treat

Quiet surprise
Change is given back
Did she somehow earn this money?

She accepts
Takes coins and her treat
She walks back home, sunshine on her face

She sits on the stairs
Calls me with good news
She made her first purchase alone

BUBBLE BOUNCE

Bubbly bounce in her walk.
Smile brightens the room.
Bubbly bounce in her voice.
Eyes sparkle with pride.
Her busy hands built boxes
everyone can find
on shelf after shelf
in round-the-corner stores.
Meaning and purpose
sprinkled on her life.
Bubbly bounce brings us beauteous bliss.

SHARING POSSIBILITIES

Someone's late for dinner,
un-responsive phone.

Maybe
        the train is late
        the bus is late
        the train collided with
                another train
                a bus
                a cargo crate.
The bus collided with
        a car
        a bus
        a fire hydrant.
Someone can't catch
        the train
        the bus
        the plane.
        The plane?
Well, yes,
why not the plane?

Someone is
        forgetful
        lost
        sick and is in
                an ambulance
                the hospital
                a cemetery.
Cemetery?
I don't think so.

Either that or
the moon.

Someone went to the moon
        for a snack
        for lunch
        for a mini vacation

and the rocket is still refueling.

Someone is

hush

Keys jangle,
slide into the lock.

The door

      creaks

         open.

            Someone

    is

home.

Bubbles Made of Circles

Wax and sand
collected
molded
under heat.
Concoction
surrounds the string
dangling in mid-air
cooled
shaved
carved
pulled slightly
here and
there.
Ready for use
un-willingly burned
remnant in my room
echo
in the fugue
grandmother
granddaughter
play.

UNIQUE FLOWER

They say you have a flower
You imagine bright red, yellow, blue
You imagine five, ten, or fifteen petals
Preconceived ideas with a long list of what to do

You hold your tiny flower
You count all the parts and pieces there
You dream of your bud's colours, shape, and texture,
Foggy future filled with hopes, dreams parents share

You watch your precious flower
You cry; desperate disbelief
Texture: rough and un-familiar
You wonder if you can find relief

You stand back from your flower
Each petal holds its own tiny stages
Previous ideas don't hold this type of beauty
Your flower grows new colours to last throughout the ages

SHARED INTERESTS

We pile into the car
just the two of us
inexplicable desire
drive far away
sit inside a car
stand outside
watch giant birds come
roundness of feet
in front of our eyes
large tails
small tails
underbellies overhead
wing spans admired
gasp at the rocking
side by side
breathe in the roars
and giant hums
we watch

minutes pass

sometimes hours

we are warmed
by the sights
we are warmed
by each other
best friends

daughter and mom

About the Author

Danielle Wong writes poetry and flash fiction. Some of her work has appeared in *Soft Cartel*, *The 2016 Poetry Marathon Anthology*, *The 2017 Poetry Marathon Anthology*, *Overture*, *Wherever We Roam*, *Waking Dawn*, and *The Warbler's Song*. She was born and raised in Saskatchewan, but lives in Montreal.

www.ingramcontent.com/pod-product-compliance
Lightning Source LLC
Chambersburg PA
CBHW032016170626
46807CB00006B/2839